Fruit of the Spirit

Fruit of the Spirit
Growth of the Heart

Bonnie Thurston

A Liturgical Press Book

 THE LITURGICAL PRESS
Collegeville, Minnesota

Cover design by Kathryn Brewer

1	2	3	4	5	6	7	8

Library of Congress Cataloging-in-Publication Data

Thurston, Bonnie Bowman.
    Fruit of the spirit : growth of the heart / Bonnie Thurston.
      p. cm.
    Includes bibliographical references.
    ISBN 0-8146-2598-3 (alk. paper)
    1. Christian Life. 2. Fruit of the Spirit—Sermons.
   3. Sermons, English. I. Title.
   BV4501.2 .T525 2000
   234'.13—dc21

                                               99-047762

In gratitude for
Marilyn Barton,
a Woman of Spirit, a Healer of Hearts

Contents

Acknowledgments

I am grateful for having had the opportunity to preach at Chautauqua August 25–29, 1998. Special thanks to Ross Mackenzie, then director of the department of religion of the Chautauqua Institution, and to Flora Mackenzie first for the kind invitation to preach at Chautauqua which led to these reflections and second for their considerable gifts of hospitality and friendship while I was in residence. My gratitude to Sheryl Thayer who answered all my questions with great grace. Jack Grigsby and his choir and Jared Jacobsen, Chautauqua organist, provided glorious music for the services, and I thank them both.

Thanks also go to the people who encouraged me to publish these sermons, and especially to James Walther, professor of New Testament at Pittsburgh Theological Seminary (now retired) who was so encouraging about the material during the week the sermons were preached and to Susan Garrett who read the printed texts so enthusiastically. My continuing gratitude goes to George Miller for his careful proofreading and to Colleen Stiller, production manager at The Liturgical Press.

A final note: sermons are oral literature and not always easily documented. Sometimes what a preacher hears or has read makes its way into his or her sermon "un-noted." I have tried to document quotations and allusions in what follows, but with mixed success. At the very least I indicate the source/author of ideas that are not my own.

Introduction

In August 1998 I was privileged to be the preacher at the Chautauqua Institution. Chautauqua is quite an experience in and of itself, and being both a "first time Chautauquan" and the preacher of the week was nearly overwhelming to a serious introvert. But everyone I met was friendly and kind. The sermons were well received (but then the people who didn't like them would hardly line up after services to say so, would they?), and several people inquired about whether I were planning to publish them. I wasn't.

Sermons are a spoken art form. I had written these reflections on the fruit of the Spirit with the idea that they were to be spoken, if truth be told, proclaimed. I came home from Chautauqua, filed the sermons in my "tasks completed" file, and went on about life. But the sermons wouldn't stay filed. Two of my colleagues at the seminary who heard the sermons thought I should publish them. A Methodist clergyman who visited us came over to my table in the refectory asking that I publish them. When, in November 1998, somebody came up to me in a bookstore in Pittsburgh to inquire about the sermons, I relented and decided to see if sermons would work as "reflections." What follows is the attempt at "trans-substantiation."

Why did I choose this subject in the first place? Probably because of the vast interest in "spirituality" in popular culture. Everybody from movie stars and politicians to corporate executives and economists seem interested in "spirituality" today. I would want to define "spirituality" broadly as "what we do about what we believe," and to suggest that the etymology of the word itself assumes an unseen world, a world of "spirit" as well as matter. That, in itself, is contrary to the materialistic and scientific orientation of most of Western society.

I don't see this interest in spirituality as a bad thing, *au contraire*. But I do think it points to the fact that we in the Church haven't done a very good job of explaining what Christianity is about. We as Church have, I think, failed to make it clear that Christianity is not limited to believing a body of doctrine (although it is that, in part). Christianity is also "what we do about what we believe." That is, Christianity has its own, distinct spirituality. The movie stars and executives who are seeking an authentic spirituality don't need to turn to Yoga or Native American religions to find a "practice." Christianity has its own set of practices. They include, but are not limited to, corporate worship, reception of the sacraments and private prayer. Historically Christian spirituality has been understood in terms of the exercise of the "virtues." And those "virtues" are clearly spelled out in Paul's letter to the churches of Galatia in his list of the "fruit of the Spirit" in 5:22-23: love, joy, peace, patience, kindness, generosity, faithfulness, gentleness, and self-control.

In the reflections which follow I suggest that Christians develop a spirituality around these "fruits" by cooperating with God both in *receiving* these fruits as gifts from the Holy Spirit (for they are, at least in part, gifts received as much as virtues cultivated) and in *exercising* them in day-to-day life. The Christian life is amphibious; it is a life of flesh and spirit, and the growth of both centers in the heart (as I explain in the first reflection) which is the center of the human person.

In the Gospels Jesus is depicted as being especially interested in the "inner life," what comes out of a person from inside. We see a case in point of this in the section of the Sermon on the Mount called the "antitheses," the "you have heard/but I say" part (Matt 5:21-48) in which Jesus is more interested in the motivation for action (anger, lust, etc.) than in behavior per se. This is because Jesus knows that what is rooted in the heart determines external action. In Galatians, Paul has embraced this basic idea.

He suggests that the Holy Spirit can fill the heart with the qualities that are manifested in deeply Christian action. The Holy Spirit offers the Christian these gifts or these fruits, and the heart grows in proportion to its ability to accept and reflect them.

In a little-known spiritual classic *Where Silence is Praise* by an anonymous Carthusian, the same idea is expressed:

> The virtues keep all our acts "ordered"—towards God, our neighbor and ourselves. This is the Christian life. The "gifts" of the Holy Spirit guide us directly; they have a direct effect; they are a higher organism which takes over as soon as all has been co-ordinated for God, and he can then do his work without encountering any obstacles in us. His least commandments are carried out, down to the tiniest fibers of our being.[1]

So, I suppose, I chose to preach on the "fruit of the Spirit" from Galatians as a way of making a small contribution to Christian spirituality, to an understanding of life from the "inside out." It didn't occur to me at the time I was preparing the sermons, but, looking at them now I note that the texts from which I preached were, with one exception, from the late first or early second century and basically of two literary forms. And both of those facts relate to our current interest in spirituality.

With the exception of Paul's letter to the churches of Galatia which was probably written between A.D. 49 and 56, or mid-first century, the other texts from which I preached were all late first or early second century documents. The letters of Peter probably come from the last quarter of the first century; the Pastoral Epistles (which include 2 Timothy) were, I think, written in the first quarter of the second century, and John was written about A.D. 90 and then "edited" between A.D. 100 and 110. "So what?" you might rightfully ask. Because the Church at the end of the first century and the beginning of the second century was facing many of the same issues that we Christians face today.

---

[1] *Where Silence is Praise* (Kalamazoo, Mich.: Cistercian Publications, 1997) 91. (While I prefer inclusive language, for accuracy I reproduce all quotations exactly as written.)

The parousia, the return of Christ, seemed to be delayed, and that meant that Christians had to learn to "live in the Empire" (live in the culture in which they found themselves). Their questions could be our own. How countercultural should we be? How much should we accommodate to the cultural norms around us? How will our answers to these questions affect our ability to share the Gospel? (Who would listen to a message preached by "weirdos"?) At the end of the first century and the beginning of the second, Christians were dealing with issues of authority (who has it and why?), with the place of women in the Church (how much "visibility" and power should they have in the Church?) and with the shocking discovery that Christians could sin! These sound very familiar. And the point is that the biblical texts from which my reflections sprang themselves arose from a context not unlike our own: from a culturally and religiously pluralistic society in which Christians were struggling to find their way.

Not surprisingly, the writers of the New Testament used literary forms that would be familiar to the first recipients of their works. The fact that they aren't always familiar to us is hardly the fault of Paul or Peter or John. As I looked over the texts from which I developed these sermons, I discovered that they either employ vice and virtue lists or a type of literature called the farewell discourse.

In Gal 5:16-25 Paul employs a rhetorical device, a "teaching tool" if you will, which he probably learned from Stoic philosophers, the vice and virtue list. Such lists were basically simple lists of "don'ts and do's" (like the "do be's" and "don't be's" of television's "Romper Room"). The "works of the flesh" in Gal 5:19-21 is basically a Stoic vice list: fornication, impurity, licentiousness, idolatry, sorcery, enmities, strife, jealousy, anger, quarrels, dissensions, factions, envy, drunkenness, carousing. These are not only behaviors of which *anyone* in the Greco-Roman world would disapprove, but they are also particularly destructive to Christian community, to the *koinonia* that should characterize Christ's followers. By contrast, the "fruit of the Spirit," to quote Paul, is a virtue list: love, joy, peace, patience, kindness, generosity, faithfulness, gentleness, and self-control. And, once again, most of these are "virtues" of which a good Hellenist would approve. Both the writer of the Petrine letters and the Pastoral letters use the same form. Second Peter 1:5-7 is basically a virtue list, and 1 Tim 6:17-19 and 2 Pet 3:8-15 enjoin widely approved behavior, patience and good works/generosity respectively.

Similarly, John 14–16 is an example of the literary form known as "farewell discourse." It is akin to the symposium, an eating and drinking party followed by the speech or instruction of a teacher. The dialogues of Plato are probably the best known example of the form. The farewell discourse was a particular type of such a speech. In Hellenistic literature we find many examples of "last meals" in which a teacher/philosopher who knows he is leaving or dying or about to be killed calls together his pupils and friends, has a last meal with them, and then gives a speech or discourse that summarizes his teaching. The dramatic setting of the teaching serves to fix it in the hearers' minds. This seems to be how John the evangelist has framed Jesus' last evening with his disciples before he is betrayed and arrested (and it may be what Luke is doing in Luke 22:24-38).

The fact that the writers of the texts on which I do expository work here were written in what were then familiar literary forms reminds me that today, as well, the Christian message is best communicated in forms widely known and used in the culture. But the fact that there turned out to be historical and literary continuity among the texts from which I preached is not the crucial issue. It is the setting forth of what I hope is a distinctively Christian spirituality. I began that task with a text from the parenetic (that is, teaching or practical exhortation) section of Paul's letter to the Galatians precisely because that text is so clear both in spelling out the "what to do," but also in communicating the fundamental theological assumption behind Christian spirituality: that it is not something we do ourselves for ourselves, but it is a participation in something which has already been done for us.

Let me explain briefly what I mean by using an admittedly crude comparison. Although it is a coarse way of thinking about it, I would suggest that in some of the Eastern religions to which many have turned for spiritual enlightenment, one "does something" for himself or herself. One practices *ahamsa* (non-injury) to gain a better rebirth, or one exercises detachment to enter *Nirvana*. Unlike in Buddhism where one is to be a "lamp unto herself," in Christianity the Light has dawned *upon* us. Christian spirituality begins as a *response* to something which is already done; one enters into a relationship that has already been restored. This is why in the Galatian letter Paul speaks of the "fruit," the already matured "product," of the Spirit which is given to those who "belong to Christ" (5:24). Those belonging to Christ are "guided by the Spirit" (5:25) and gifted by the Spirit with those qualities ("fruits") that characterize the inner life of God. They are to accept, internalize, and exercise those gifts.

The implications of all this are the subject of the reflections that follow. For your convenience, a relevant psalm and the text from which the reflection is taken are provided (both in the New Revised Standard Version). It is best to read "Fruit of the Spirit, Desires of the Heart" first. Thereafter the reflections can be read in any order. At Chautauqua I began each sermon with the following prayer. It is, as well, my prayer for those who read these reflections.

> O God Who knows the secrets of our hearts, may it please you to give all people increase of grace to hear, receive and respond to your Word. May we bring forth in our lives the fruit of the Spirit, for we ask it in the name of him who manifested their perfection, even Jesus Christ the Lord. Amen.

January 2, 1999
St. Basil the Great and St. Gregory Nazianzen

Fruit of the Spirit, Desires of the Heart

Psalm 63:1-8

> O God, you are my God, I seek you,
> my soul thirsts for you;
> my flesh faints for you,
> as in a dry and weary land where there is no water.
> So I have looked upon you in the sanctuary,
> beholding your power and glory.
> Because your steadfast love is better than life,
> my lips will praise you.
> So I will bless you as long as I live;
> I will lift up my hands and call upon your name.
>
> My soul is satisfied as with a rich feast,
> and my mouth praises you with joyful lips
> when I think of you on my bed,
> and meditate on you in the watches of the night;
> for you have been my help,
> and in the shadow of your wings I sing for joy.
> My soul clings to you;
> your right hand upholds me.

Galatians 5:16-25

Live by the Spirit, I say, and do not gratify the desires of the flesh. For what the flesh desires is opposed to the Spirit, and what the Spirit desires is opposed to the flesh; for these are opposed to each other, to prevent you from doing what you want. But if you are led by the Spirit, you are not subject to the law. Now the works of the flesh are obvious: fornication, impurity, licentiousness, idolatry, sorcery, enmities, strife, jealousy, anger, quarrels, dissensions, factions, envy, drunkenness, carousing, and things like these. I am warning you, as I warned you before: those who do such things will not inherit the kingdom of God.

By contrast, the fruit of the Spirit is love, joy, peace, patience, kindness, generosity, faithfulness, gentleness, and self-control. There is no law against such things. And those who belong to Christ Jesus have crucified the flesh with its passions and desires. If we live by the Spirit, let us also be guided by the Spirit.

Be of good cheer. What follows is not a panegyric on the virtues of the Spirit at the expense of the flesh. This is, in fact, a reflection on desire, a word which I should like to see reclaimed as wholesome and central to the formation of the Christian person.

A sermon on desire is consistent with Paul's most passionate epistle, his letter to the churches of Galatia. The apostle is beside himself because the Galatian Christians are deserting the Gospel he has brought them. His agitation is everywhere apparent in the letter. Uncharacteristically, it has no thanksgiving (he isn't, at the moment, thankful for them!). He addresses his converts as "foolish Galatians" and goes so far as to call them "bewitched" (3:1). In a passage I certainly wouldn't introduce in Sunday School, Paul suggests the male members of the community perform radical surgery on themselves (see Gal 5:12).

All this belies the oft presented view of Paul as a wizened judge, a bloodless theologian. Here he is a parent frantic for his children. Indeed, he describes himself as a mother: "My little children, for whom I am again in the pain of childbirth until Christ is formed in you, I wish I were present with you now and could change my tone, for I am perplexed about you" (4:19-20).

Paul's perplexity is an issue of the heart. Paul's own heart goes out to the Galatian Christians; he knows that the arena of the heart is the arena of desire. As the heart goes, so goes the person. The language of our text contrasts the desires of the flesh and the desires of the Spirit, but at issue is the desires of the heart. False teaching in Galatia has led to false desires. The hearts of Paul's children in Galatia are being led astray.

For Paul and for the writers of the New Testament, the heart was the center of the person. In scripture "heart" is a metaphor for the whole person, for the centrality of being. When the psalmist writes "Search me, O God, and know my heart" (139:23), he is asking God to examine the very essence of his being. Similarly when he asks that God "Create in me a clean heart" (51:10), he is asking that his very self be purified. When the psalmist asks that God "grant you your heart's desire" (20:4), he is asking that God grant the deepest yearnings of the person.

To speak of the heart is to speak of the deepest part of ourselves, the center of our freedom and responsibility. It is the land of our longing. The heart's desire is that which, with the inner self, the essential or most vital part of the person, one longs for, yearns for, is attracted to. Desire is a perfectly good word. It speaks of the strength and vigor of our emotional life. It moves us toward the future, for desire is an impulse toward something which we do not yet have, something which promises to be pleasurable and good—or we wouldn't desire it. Gregory the Great called desire the language of the soul.

In the fascinating book *Befriending Our Desires*, Philip Sheldrake says that "desires are best understood as our most honest experiences of ourselves, in all our complexity and depth, as we relate to people and things around us."[1] Desire speaks to us of what we do not have and thus opens us to possibility and to the future. Desire, in short, is an animating principle in life.

---

[1] Philip Sheldrake, *Befriending Our Desires* (Notre Dame, Ind.: Ave Maria Press, 1994) 12.

Sexual appetite is only one example of animating desire. Desires of the heart are much more profound and consuming. This is reflected in the Greek verb *desire, epithumeo,* which is formed from *epi,* to or towards, and *thumos,* intense feeling, even anger. Heat. Desire is about heat. What warms us. What can, in fact, literally consume us. As is the heart's desire, so is the person. And that, of course, is the issue. What is our heart's desire? To what do we give our hearts?

The heart is that in us which is directed to the Other. For the Christian to live from the desire of the heart is to live from a deep and powerful longing for the ultimate Other, for God, and this is what makes us different, and why our heart's desire can be so positive. When St. Augustine wrote that our hearts are restless until they find rest in God, he wrote of desire as it should function. He wrote in concert with the psalmist who cries out to God,

> And there is nothing on earth that I desire other than you.
> My flesh and my heart may fail,
>> but God is the strength of my heart and my portion
>> forever (73:25-26).

My favorite expression of this longing, this desire of the heart for God, comes from Psalm 42:

> As a deer longs for flowing streams,
>> so my soul longs for you, O God.
> My soul thirsts for God,
>> for the living God (42:1-2).

The desire for God is physical, a great thirst in a dry place. What are you thirsty for? What is your heart's desire? It is a crucial question for you are formed in the image of what you desire.

This is why Paul warns the Galatians against the "works" of the flesh. Note the flesh, itself, is not evil, but its works do not fulfill the deepest longing of the human heart, the heart made in God's image. Idolatry and magic, jealousy and anger, sex and drink, these do not fulfill the heart, because they are not the stuff of which the heart is made. This passage opens with a contrast between what the flesh desires and what the Spirit desires, and the Spirit's desires become "fruit." Singular. All these lovely virtues which we shall be considering—love, joy, peace, patience, kindness, generosity, faithfulness, gentleness, self-control—*together* are the "fruit of the Spirit." Paul wants us to desire this fruit because it is what characterizes God. The desires of the heart must be for what and who God is. Nothing else will ultimately satisfy or satisfy ultimately. "All that falls short of God," says Dame Julian of Norwich, "will never satisfy us."[2]

We must grow beyond the works and desires of the flesh. Flesh is good, created by God to be so. But it and its works are temporal. "All people are grass," as the prophet Isaiah reminds us, and "like the flower of the field" that withers (Isa 40:6-7). Its desires are not heart desires, not the yearnings for eternity, for the One who made it. This is what Paul is getting at when he says that "those who belong to Christ Jesus have crucified the flesh with its passions and desires" (v. 24). Through participation in the death and resurrection of Jesus through baptism, Christians are ushered into the very life of God. And even one small and partial taste of that life creates an enormous appetite for itself.

Any desires that are for less than the characteristics of God, than for God's very self will not satisfy because, ultimately, we are made to be like God. Meister Eckhart, the medieval German mystic who was frequently in trouble for his way of putting things (and in this he has my sympathy!), said that "we are all meant to be Mothers of God, for God is always needing to be born." We Christians are made by God to be little Gods, or, more precisely, little Christs. This is the process which Orthodox or Eastern Christianity calls "deification in Christ." It is what the fourteenth-century English mystic Walter

---

[2] John Skinner (trans.), *Revelation of Love, Julian of Norwich* (New York: Doubleday/Image, 1996) 10.

Hilton called reforming the image of God in the human soul. It begins with the fact that we are made in the image and likeness of God. "Then God said, 'let us make humankind in our image, according to our likeness. . . . So God created humankind in his image, in the image of God he created them; male and female he created them" (Gen 2:26, 27). How profound is this truth set forth by the writer of Genesis! And how profoundly it affects our desires!

Because I think this Genesis passage speaks the truth, that we are made in the Divine Image, it is my suspicion that all our hearts' desires are, in one way or another, however twisted and devious, desires for God. Sexual desire, with all its physical force, with its urge toward power, with its tenderness and giving, is, at root, a desire for reunion with the Other, for overcoming a primal estrangement, and for the creativity and generativity of God that issues forth in new life. Desire for power or for wealth are really desire for modes of control, desire to assume that god-like role. Desire for beauty is desire to reflect God who is the source of beauty. Desire for wisdom and knowledge is desire to be like the One who is all wisdom and knowledge.

Maximus the Confessor puts the matter philosophically: "If all things have been made by God . . . then God is better than what has been made," he notes. "The one who forsakes the better and is engrossed in inferior things shows that he prefers the things made by God to God." Maximus is right; we have wandered a long way from God and lost sight of the fact that the deepest desires of our hearts are for the attributes of God, for all the fruit of the Spirit shows forth aspects of God. The desires of our hearts must ultimately be desires for God. This is not a new insight. In the sixth century B.C. the prophet Ezekiel understood it. Through him God spoke of the renewal of Israel in terms of the cleansing of the heart. ". . . I will cleanse you," God says, "A new heart I will give you, and a new spirit I will put within you; and I will remove from your body the heart of stone and give you a heart of flesh. I will put my spirit within you. . . ." (Ezek 36:25-27).

And how did God do this for God's willful and wandering people? Through Jesus the Christ. The first letter of Peter explains, "Christ suffered for sins once for all . . . in order to bring us to God. He was put to death in the flesh, but made alive in the spirit" (3:18). Jesus came to bring the heart of God among us in the flesh, to show us what the desires of the *real* heart look like, to show us what desires our hearts should grow toward, what fruit we should bring forth. Christ himself appointed us to bear that fruit, lasting fruit. ". . . I appointed you to go and bear fruit, fruit that will last" (John 15:16).

The authentic desires of the Christian's heart are for the fruit of the Spirit, for the attributes of God shown most clearly in Jesus Christ, for God alone. "Whom have I in heaven but you?" asks the psalmist, "And there is nothing on earth that I desire other than you" (73:25). AMEN and AMEN.

2

Faithfulness, Gentleness, Self-Control

Psalm 103:1-5, 8-22

> Bless the LORD, O my soul,
>> and all that is within me,
>> bless his holy name.
> Bless the LORD, O my soul,
>> and do not forget all his benefits—
> who forgives all your iniquity,
>> who heals all your diseases,
> who redeems your life from the Pit,
>> who crowns you with steadfast love and mercy,
> who satisfies you with good as long as you live
>> so that your youth is renewed like the eagle's. . . .
>
> The LORD is merciful and gracious,
>> slow to anger and abounding in steadfast love.
> He will not always accuse,
>> nor will he keep his anger forever.
> He does not deal with us according to our sins,
>> nor repay us according to our iniquities.
> For as the heavens are high above the earth,
>> so great is his steadfast love toward those who fear him;
> as far as the east is from the west,
>> so far he removes our transgressions from us.
> As a father has compassion for his children,
>> so the LORD has compassion for those who fear him.
> For he knows how we were made;
>> he remembers that we are dust.

As for mortals, their days are like grass;
　　they flourish like a flower of the field;
for the wind passes over it, and it is gone,
　　and its place knows it no more.
But the steadfast love of the LORD is from everlasting
　　　to everlasting
　　on those who fear him,
　　and his righteousness to children's children,
to those who keep his covenant
　　and remember to do his commandments.

The LORD has established his throne in the heavens,
　　and his kingdom rules over all.
Bless the LORD, O you his angels,
　　you mighty ones who do his bidding,
　　obedient to his spoken word.
Bless the LORD, all his hosts,
　　his ministers that do his will.
Bless the LORD, all his works,
　　in all places of his dominion.
Bless the LORD, O my soul.

2 Peter 1:3-11

His divine power has given us everything needed for life and godliness, through the knowledge of him who called us by his own glory and goodness. Thus he has given us, through these things his precious and very great promises, so that through them you may escape from the corruption that is in the world because of lust, and may become participants of the divine nature. For this very reason, you must make every effort to support your faith with goodness, and goodness with knowledge, and knowledge with self-control, and self-control with endurance, and endurance with godliness, and godliness with mutual affection, and mutual affection with love. For if these things are yours and are increasing among you, they keep you from being ineffective and unfruitful in the knowledge of our Lord Jesus Christ. For anyone who lacks these things is nearsighted and blind, and is forgetful of the cleansing of past sins. Therefore, brothers and sisters, be all the more eager to confirm your call and election, for if you do this, you will never stumble. For in this way, entry into the eternal kingdom of our Lord and Savior Jesus Christ will be richly provided for you.

On the morning of May 31, 1997 after a roaring windstorm the night before, I took a small boat from the village of Kas in Turkey to Teimassa via what is called the "sunken city of Kekova." Until the wind picked up again in the afternoon, it was all the Mediterranean is supposed to be: a dramatic, rocky coastline, deep aquamarine water as smooth as the surface of a mirror, a sky blue enough to wrap the Blessed Virgin Mary. We passed many little inlets and peninsulas of the sort that made piracy a major industry along this coast in antiquity.

The fishermen who owned the boat were rugged looking, and handsome. They smoked and sailed and, as we putted unhurriedly along, talked and told an amazing story which was translated for me. One day when they were out fishing, a dolphin came alongside their boat. It jumped and thumped against the boat, and they became quite clear that it wanted to tell them something. As it turned out, when they reeled in their net, they had caught the dolphin's mate and inadvertently killed it.

Turkish fishermen are close to the sea and to its creatures which sustain them, and they were very sad about their mistake. And because of their closeness, their relatedness to the sea and its creatures, they told the dolphin who had followed them what had happened. They spoke to it as if it were human, and apologized profusely for the terrible thing they had unknowingly done. The dolphin that had been with them all that long day dove deep into the blue of the sea. And they never saw it come up for air. They believe it committed suicide, that this gentle creature in its faithfulness had the self-control to join its lost mate.

Faithfulness. Gentleness. Self-control. My point is not that the best manifestation of these virtues is seen in suicide. It is that these are not attributes that will foster what is called "getting on in the world." They aren't virtues that will make us rich and famous. We won't find the terms discussed in the manuals that business wonks write to help anxious middle-managers rise to the top of corporations. You won't read in *Forbes* or *Fortune* or *Money* magazines that the three habits of successful executives and the fabulously wealthy are faithfulness, gentleness, and self-control. Our highest public officials seldom evince these traits in public or private.

"Faithfulness," *pistis* in Greek, was the common, secular word for trustworthiness, for fidelity, especially fidelity to standards of truth. Oddly apropos of the dolphin story, St. Jerome explained that it was the trust in persons because of their love. "Gentleness," *prautes*, is nearly untranslatable. At its root is a word that was used of animals that were tamed and under control. In the New Testament it describes those who are submissive to God's will, whose mildness in dealing with others reflects their willingness to submit themselves to God. It is the word which is translated "meek" in the beatitude: "Blessed are the meek, (the gentle) for they will inherit the earth" (Matt 5:5). And it is what Jesus says of himself when he says "I am gentle and humble of heart" (Matt 11:29). "Self-control," *egkrateia*, is used by Plato in the *Republic* of one who has achieved self mastery. In the New Testament, it is perfectly manifested in Christ Jesus whose desires were the desires of God.

Faithfulness, gentleness, and self-control are not personality traits designed to make one effective and successful or rich and famous, but those who cultivate them mirror the God whom they describe. Faithful, gentle, self-controlled: this is our God. As the psalmist understood, God is a God of faithful love: "The Lord is merciful and gracious, slow to anger and abounding in steadfast love" (103:8). This God forgives, heals, redeems, crowns with love and mercy, satisfies with good because this is a God of faithfulness, gentleness, self-control. This is a God of perfect fidelity and self-mastery, a God who absorbs into the Divine Self all the anger that could rightly be directed at creation, a God who absorbs wrath and suffers because the Divine Essence is *hesed,* faithful love.

The first letter of Peter reminds us this same God has given us everything needed for life and godliness and for this reason we are to make every effort to support our faith with goodness and our goodness with knowledge and our knowledge with self-control and our self-control with [faithfulness or] endurance and our endurance with godliness, and our godliness with mutual affection and our mutual affection with love (1 Pet 1:3, 5-7). Because of who God is, we are to make every effort to be like God.

"The heavens are telling the glory of God," the psalmist proclaims, "and the firmament proclaims [God's] handiwork" (19:1). In its purity, all God's creation reflects God. Gentleness. Faithfulness. Self-control. The psalmist also reminds us that God has given *us* dominion over "the fish of the sea, and whatever passes along the paths of the sea" (Ps 8:8). If the fish of the sea and the mammals who ply the deep waters can mirror their maker, is it so much to ask of us, God's creatures of earth and air?

3

Kindness and Generosity

Psalm 33

Rejoice in the LORD, O you righteous.
  Praise befits the upright.
Praise the LORD with the lyre;
  make melody to him with the harp of ten strings.
Sing to him a new song;
  play skillfully on the strings, with loud shouts.

For the word of the LORD is upright,
  and all his work is done in faithfulness.
He loves righteousness and justice;
  the earth is full of the steadfast love of the LORD.

By the word of the LORD the heavens were made,
  and all their host by the breath of his mouth.
He gathered the waters of the sea as in a bottle,
  he put the deeps in storehouses.
Let all the earth fear the LORD;
  let all the inhabitants of the world stand in awe of him.
For he spoke, and it came to be;
  he commanded and it stood firm.

The LORD brings the counsel of the nations to nothing;
  he frustrates the plans of the peoples.
The counsel of the LORD stands forever,
  the thoughts of his heart to all generations.
Happy is the nation whose God is the LORD,
  the people whom he has chosen as his heritage.

The LORD looks down from heaven;
    he sees all humankind.
From where he sits enthroned he watches
    all the inhabitants of the earth—
he who fashions the hearts of them all,
    and observes all their deeds.
A king is not saved by his great army;
    a warrior is not delivered by his great strength.
The war horse is a vain hope for victory,
    and by its great might it cannot save.

Truly the eye of the LORD is on those who fear him,
    on those who hope in his steadfast love,
to deliver their soul from death,
    and to keep them alive in famine.

Our soul waits for the LORD;
    he is our help and shield.
Our heart is glad in him,
    because we trust in his holy name.
Let your steadfast love, O LORD, be upon us,
    even as we hope in you.

1 Timothy 6:17-19

As for those who in the present age are rich, command them not to be haughty, or to set their hopes on the uncertainty of riches, but rather on God who richly provides us with everything for our enjoyment. They are to do good, to be rich in good works, generous, and ready to share, thus storing up for themselves the treasure of a good foundation for the future, so that they may take hold of the life that is really life.

Many people seem to be lamenting the loss of what might be called "common courtesy" in day-to-day life. Yale law professor Stephen Carter's recent book *Civility: Manners, Morals, and the Etiquette of Democracy* decries this loss of civility in American society, the loss of respect for others and of the need, as he puts it, "to show generosity even when it may be costly, and trust even when there is risk." His conclusion is that only a religious understanding of the world can counter the prevailing cultural trends of impropriety, disrespect, and self-ishness.[1] Professor Carter's is a cry that people should be a good deal more than "nice."

I thought of this because I was recently involved in a conversation in which it was lamented that "being nice" and "being Christian" are so often mistakenly equated. Personally, I've never liked the word "nice," as its Old French root means "stupid," and its Latin root means "ignorant." At best it's an insipid term. However, I thought the point was well taken. Many people do think that "being Christian" means that one must be "nice," that is, agreeable, pleasant, thoughtful, well-mannered, the sort of person who wouldn't upset the social status quo; the sort of person who knows which fork to use in a good restaurant; the sort of person who is acceptable in, well, "nice" company.

The writer of 1 Timothy was more than a little concerned that the recipients of his letter be "nice," that is, be acceptable in terms defined by the society in which they found themselves. He tells them to pray for "kings and all who are in high positions" "so that we may lead a quiet and peaceable life" (2:2). Christian women are to be quiet and submissive, because that was the dominant role for "nice" women in his society ("ladies" as they were called in my youth) (2:11). Bishops are to be "respectable" (3:2), "well thought of by outsiders" (3:7). I could give other examples, but the point for me is that in the Pastoral Epistles (1 and 2 Timothy and Titus) we see the beginnings of the Church's unfortunate tendency to sell out the Gospel in favor of being "nice" in society's eyes.

Christ calls his people to be a good deal more than "nice." He calls us to give our life for others. And he washed feet and

---

[1] Quoted in Jane Lampman, "Fostering Trust and Civility Is a Moral Issue," *The Christian Science Monitor* (May 28, 1998) B-3.

died on a cross to show us what this might mean. By his cross and resurrection, Jesus empowers us to be profoundly virtuous, to receive (for they are gifts, not human accomplishments) the very virtues that characterize the inner life of God: Love, Joy, Peace, Patience, Kindness, Generosity, Faithfulness, Gentleness, Self-Control. And this brings us around to the subject of this reflection: Kindness and Generosity.

Interestingly, in both English and Greek there is little difference between the two words. In English both have roots that mean "type" or "group of" as in the Latin *genus*. One who is kind is gentle, benevolent, and generous. One who is generous is kind, gracious, giving. And so it is in Greek. One finds little difference between the dictionary definitions of the words. Kindness, *chrestotes*, is defined as "goodness" or "sweetness." It is a word that classical writers chose to describe excellence of character. It is a word that secular Greek used to describe old wine, wine that was mellow (my favorite miracle of Jesus was that done at the wedding feast at Cana!).

Interestingly, "kind" is literally the word that Jesus used to describe the nature of his yoke in Matt 11:30. Our translations read, "my yoke is easy" but the word is literally "kind" in the sense of "comfortable" or "fitting for the work to be done," "tailor made," so to speak. "Generosity," *agathosune* in Greek, is defined as "goodness" with the implication being more active than that of "kindness." Generosity in Greek is beneficence, kindness showing itself in action. This is why Paul uses the term in the Ephesian letter when he says that "the fruit of light is found in all that is good" (5:9).

And that put me in mind of another conversation I heard, a story that was related. A very young family had struggled through the diagnosis of cancer with their small daughter. The child was about five years old and had endured many surgeries, many treatments, and chemotherapy that had left her bald. But her prognosis was good, and the family decided to go out to dinner to celebrate. They didn't choose an elegant restaurant, but they chose a good one. Of course, they were worried about how people would react to their active, cheerful, bald daughter. They thought a better class of people, nicer people, might be found in a better restaurant. You know, people less likely to stare. So they dressed up and went out for their party.

It was a good choice of restaurant, subdued, slightly darkened, pleasant. The hostess didn't bat an eye as she seated the family. The waiter brought the menus, rattled off the specials and didn't stare. The family chose their dinners. The bread and salads appeared and then . . . yes, you guessed it, the little girl had to go to the restroom. Most of us have faced it, the long walk across the dining room with a child in tow. So the mother got up with the daughter. The very attractive, even elegant lady at the next table smiled kindly as they passed.

Off they went to the ladies' room, and they accomplished the business at hand. But as they were leaving the restroom, the lady from the next table came in. She knelt down by the little bald girl and said, "You've had cancer, haven't you?" "Oh, no," thought the child's mother, "now what?" and she prepared to go into her protective mode (you know it, mothers, the Protective Mode). But the elegant lady continued, "me, too. And I'm bald, too." At which point she removed her hairdo and plopped it down on the little girl's head. The child was delighted. She raced to the full-length mirror as the two older women grinned and told her how lovely she looked. The women had a conversation about cancer and recovery while the little girl giggled delightedly and played with the wig. After a time, they all returned to their tables. The elegant lady winked at her escort and resumed her dinner.

But the little girl couldn't wait to tell her Dad what had happened and how grown up she looked in the wig. And before her mother could either explain or stop her, she had slipped off her chair, hopped over to the elegant lady's table and asked, "may I borrow your hair to show my Dad?"

Picture it now . . . The nice restaurant. The attractive clientele. The elegant lady and her escort. "May I borrow your hair to show my Dad?" And as the little girl's horrified mother looked on, the elegant lady took off her lovely wig and placed it carefully on the little girl's head. "Go show your Daddy, sweetheart."

"The fruit of light is found in all that is good" (Eph 5:9). This wasn't just "nice." It is what Carter called "generosity even when it [is] costly." It was "good" in the way that the writer of 1 Timothy meant it. "They . . . are to be rich in good works, generous, and ready to share, . . . so that they may take hold of the life that is really life" (6:18-19). The elegant lady in the restaurant really knew how to live . . . and that was manifested in much more than fine dining. She knew that life in its fullness comes not from self-actualization (as the '60s psychologists would tell us), but from self-transcendence (as Christ on the cross shows us). Her action incarnated Christ's words, "those who lose their life for my sake will find it" (Matt 10:39).

Her kindness was manifested in the generosity that comes from real love, the love that is Jesus Christ among us. Greater love has no elegant woman than this: that she take off her hair for an anonymous little bald girl. AMEN.

Patience

Psalm 37:1-9

Do not fret because of the wicked;
    do not be envious of wrongdoers,
for they will soon fade like the grass,
    and wither like the green herb.

Trust in the LORD and do good;
    so you will live in the land, and enjoy security.
Take delight in the LORD,
    and he will give you the desires of your heart.

Commit your way to the LORD;
    trust in him, and he will act.
He will make your vindication shine like the light,
    and the justice of your cause like the noonday.

Be still before the LORD, and wait patiently for him;
    do not fret over those who prosper in their way,
    over those who carry out evil devices.

Refrain from anger, and forsake wrath.
    Do not fret—it leads only to evil.
For the wicked shall be cut off,
    but those who wait for the LORD shall inherit the land.

2 Peter 3:8-15a

But do not ignore this one fact, beloved, that with
the Lord one day is like a thousand years, and a thousand

years are like one day. The Lord is not slow about his promise, as some think of slowness, but is patient with you, not wanting any to perish, but all to come to repentance. But the day of the Lord will come like a thief, and then the heavens will pass away with a loud noise, and the elements will be dissolved with fire, and the earth and everything that is done on it will be disclosed.

Since all these things are to be dissolved in this way, what sort of persons ought you to be in leading lives of holiness and godliness, waiting for and hastening the coming of the day of God, because of which the heavens will be set ablaze and dissolved, and the elements will melt with fire? But in accordance with his promise, we wait for new heavens and a new earth, where righteousness is at home.

Therefore, beloved, while you are waiting for these things, strive to be found by him at peace, without spot or blemish; and regard the patience of our Lord as salvation.

You are standing in a long line at the grocery checkout aisle. There are three people with full carts in front of you. You have forty-five minutes to finish your shopping, get home and get dinner started because your family has a commitment at church tonight. The "checker" is new and slow, having to stop frequently to confirm prices. Ah, but this is your lucky afternoon. The aisle to your left has just opened up. The man behind you in line has only three items. He goes into the new aisle ahead of you and you follow. This will be a piece of cake. Not. He pulls out a checkbook to pay for his items as the checker goes to see if she can find the store manager to approve the check. Patience.

You have been in traffic for forty-five minutes. You left home in plenty of time to make your flight, but you didn't anticipate this traffic. But, never mind, you are fourth in line at the stoplight, and one left turn away from the freeway that you can see is clear. If you make this light you will surely also make your plane. This will be a piece of cake. Not. Two cars ahead of you, the car stalls and the driver doesn't know what to do as the turn signal goes from green to yellow to red, green to yellow to red. Patience.

Patience, we are told, is a virtue. But it is a virtue that is hard for us third-millennium Americans because it involves waiting. And we don't want to wait. We want it all now. We want food that can be microwaved in thirty seconds. We want microchips that make our computers work faster than our brains can think. We want faster automobiles. Many in my generation want the financial wherewithal now that it took our parents a lifetime to accrue. We don't want to wait, not at the grocer's or in traffic or at all.

But life isn't like that. It involves various kinds of waiting, waiting that is for our own good. We might as well develop patience because for some things we are going to have to wait. The writer of the Petrine epistles understood this very clearly. He is writing to a community suffering many trials and afflictions. What they are waiting for is either more severe difficulties or deliverance. Like most Christians of the first generation, they looked forward to an imminent parousia, the return of the Lord Jesus Christ in glory to right the wrongs that they lived with. But they are being asked to wait for the Lord's deliverance which, they are told, will come in God's own time (I wonder if that weren't cold comfort since that delay might well mean that many of them would be martyred first). At this point, the text from 2 Peter makes two points that help us to understand why patience, also translated persistence, forbearance, and long-suffering, is such an important fruit of the Spirit.

First, the writer of 2 Peter understands that God's time is not like our time. His premise is, to use the words of a popular hymn, that "God is working His purpose out as year succeeds to year." But it's humans that experience "years," not God. "Beloved," he writes, "with the Lord one day is like a thousand years, and a thousand years are like one day" (v. 8). Jesus, son of Sirach, a Jewish sage writing in Jerusalem in the second century

B.C. had already articulated the point. "The number of a man's years is great," he writes, "if he reaches a hundred years. Like a drop of water from the sea and a grain of sand so are a few years in the day of eternity. Therefore the Lord is patient with [us] and pours out his mercy upon [us]" (Wisdom of Jesus ben Sirach 18:9-11).

We experience time in a linear fashion: yesterday, today, tomorrow or morning, noon, night or past, present, future. God's time isn't like that. Being omniscient, all-knowing, for God all time is present. God holds all time in a moment of time. God's benevolent purposes for us "are" right this moment in the mind of God, but they may be in the category of "to be" (future tense) for us. For quite good reasons this involves waiting for us, and it certainly involves more attentiveness to the present moment since it is, first, the only moment we have for sure, and, second, the locus of God's activity, the "place" where we will meet God. Waiting asks us to be "present tense" people.

And that is the second thing that was so clear to ben Sirach and to the writer of 2 Peter. The delay of God's activity on our behalf is for a purpose. Indeed, it is, he thinks, for our own good. He articulates it this way. "The Lord is not slow about his promise, as some think of slowness, but is patient with you, not wanting any to perish, but all to come to repentance" (v. 9). "Regard the patience of our Lord as salvation" (v. 15). The writer of 2 Peter has come to have something of the mind of the Lord. He sees the "big picture," as it were, and knows that if "the day of the Lord" comes immediately, many will perish.

Many biblical scholars think that it was the evangelist Luke who first understood that the parousia would be delayed and that the delay was for a purpose, that purpose being spreading the Gospel of Jesus Christ, enlarging the kingdom's citizenry. The delay of Christ's return is so that many more people can be called to salvation via the Gospel. Our epistle puts it succinctly: "Regard the patience of our Lord as salvation" (15a). The Lord's patience means salvation.

What would have become of us if God were not patient

with us? All of salvation history is, I would suggest, the history of God's patience. God chooses the patriarchs and matriarchs and is patient when they are disobedient. God leads the Hebrews out of Egypt and is patient when they apostatize in the desert (with a little intercession from Moses, to be sure). God gives Israel the kings she calls for and is patient when they make a muck of things. God gives the prophets to remind the Chosen of who and whose they are, and instead of severing relationship with us when we ignored those prophets, God manifested the Divine Life among us in the person of Jesus of Nazareth.

Over and over again in the New Testament, patience is the term used to describe the attitude of God toward humanity. In his first letter to them, Peter reminded the churches that "God waited patiently in the days of Noah, during the building of the ark," so that eight people could be saved (1 Pet 3:20). Writing to the church at Rome, Paul asks rhetorically, "do you despise the riches of [God's] kindness and forbearance and patience?" (2:4). Unfortunately, we often do. Paul goes on to put the matter quite directly in chapter nine of that letter, "God . . . has endured with much patience the objects of wrath" (9:22). God has, in short, endured us.

Christian people are called to be patient because God is patient. Greek dictionaries define the word "patience" with the phrase "enduring exasperating conduct without anger." St. John Chrysostom described patience as the grace of one who could revenge himself and does not. Certainly this describes God who absorbs into the Divine Self the anger and revenge that might rightly, and even justly, be directed at us. And that patience means salvation for us because it gives us time to grow, to mature in heart, to become the people that God intends for us to be and empowers us to be through the gift of the Holy Spirit at baptism.

The words of Psalm 37 might well be the words of Peter to his suffering churches: "Trust in the LORD, and do good" (v. 3); "Commit your way to the LORD; trust in him, and he will act" (v. 5). "Be still before the LORD, and wait patiently for him" (v. 7). He does ask rhetorically, "what sort of persons ought you to be in leading lives of holiness and godliness, waiting for and hastening the coming of the day of God?" (2 Pet 3:11). If God is patient, he asks, shouldn't you be? "Therefore, beloved," he continues, "while you are waiting . . . strive to be found by [God] at peace. . . ." (2 Pet 3:14).

This brings us back to where we began: We aren't patient because we don't like to wait. But waiting in the Greek language is not enduring in its passive sense. No, indeed, "waiting" in these two verses are present active participles, "doing words." The word for waiting in Greek literally means "to think toward" or "to imagine toward." To "wait" for something as Peter uses the term means to await it expectantly, to look forward to it, to expect it, indeed, to hope for it.

As our hearts grow, we will come to understand that, as a fruit of the Spirit, patience is intrinsically related to hope. We can wait, we can be patient because we trust the One in whom we hope. Benedictine Br. David Steindl-Rast has written that hope is openness to surprise, and "pure hope expects the surprise that even the worst, if it happens, will be the best. And pure grateful hope is never disappointed in this expectation."[1] In the great eighth chapter of Romans, the apostle Paul put it this way: "For in hope we were saved. Now hope that is seen is not hope. For who hopes for [or who "awaits" as some manuscript traditions have it] what is seen? But if we hope for what we do not see, we wait for it with patience" (8:24-25).

So be it. AMEN.

---

[1] David Steindl-Rast, *Gratefulness, the Heart of Prayer* (New York: Paulist Press, 1984) 143.

Peace

Psalm 23

> The LORD is my shepherd, I shall not want.
>> He makes me lie down in green pastures;
> he leads me beside still waters;
>> he restores my soul.
> He leads me in right paths
>> for his name's sake.
>
> Even though I walk through the darkest valley,
>> I fear no evil;
> for you are with me;
>> your rod and your staff—
>> they comfort me.
>
> You prepare a table before me
>> in the presence of my enemies;
> you anoint my head with oil;
>> my cup overflows.
> Surely goodness and mercy shall follow me
>> all the days of my life,
> and I shall dwell in the house of the LORD
>> my whole life long.

John 14:25-27

"I have said these things to you while I am still with you. But the Advocate, the Holy Spirit, whom the Father will send in my name, will teach you everything, and remind you of all that I have said to you. Peace I leave with you; my peace I give to you. I do not give to you as the world gives. Do not let your hearts be troubled, and do not let them be afraid."

We are embarking in the last three meditations on what is perhaps the sweetest fruit of the Spirit: Peace, Joy, and Love. Peace, joy, and love are things we want for our children and long for ourselves. They are the qualities that characterize those of mature heart. And they are not as popularly understood to be.

I grew up in a marvelous Campbellite church in Southern West Virginia. We had, in good Campbellite fashion, "no creed but Christ, no book but the Bible." It is a great heritage. While we didn't have a fancy liturgy or recite the Nicean Creed on Sundays, we could sing. In fact, as I reflect on it, we sang our theology. And so I began to think about "peace songs" as a way of entering into the meaning of "peace," not the peace songs of my '60s youth, but of my '50s childhood. What a fascinating path it led me down!

The first song that came to mind we learned in Vacation Bible School. (VBS was a very big deal in my home church. We loved it!) Like most VBS songs it has, you guessed it, hand motions. "I've got peace like a river; I've got peace like a river; I've got peace like a river in my soul;" sung with hands wagging in wave-like patterns. The second song that came to mind was more serious. "It is Well with My Soul," that wonderful collaboration by nineteenth-century Middle East missionaries Horatio Spafford of Jerusalem and Philip Bliss of Beirut, begins

> When peace, like a river, attendeth my way,
> when sorrows like sea billows roll;
> whatever my lot, thou hast taught me to say,
> it is well, it is well with my soul.

Interestingly, in both songs, peace is associated with rivers. But here again my early experience kicks in. In southern West Virginia we have precious little experience with "peaceful rivers." Our mighty New River cut a gorge right down through the mountains, and its white-water rafting trips are now a major source of tourism for us. One doesn't white-water raft on a peaceful river. The wide Ohio River marked a serious boundary to the west. The Kanawha and Guyandot rivers were notorious for flooding. Our rivers aren't peaceful. What gives? How can peace be like a river?

The writer of the Sunday school song and Horatio Spafford understood, I think, what the Lord Jesus Christ meant when he said, "Peace I leave with you; my peace I give to you. I do not give to you as the world gives" (14:27). "I do not give to you as the world gives" is a crucial and often overlooked sentence. What it means is that the peace that is such a sweet fruit of the Spirit is not as Webster would have it "freedom from . . . strife," "freedom from public disturbance," "freedom from hostility." But it is "an undisturbed state of mind; serenity" often *in the face of* strife, disturbance, and hostility.

Notice in the very brief text from John that this peace is not something manufactured by a human being, but that it is a gift given by Jesus: "*My* peace I *give* you," he says. Peace here in John's Gospel is literally a gift of the Spirit, the Advocate (or Counselor). It originates with God and comes to us, via the Holy Spirit, as gift (remember this, if you will, when you read the next chapter on joy). It is related to the hope at the root of patience that we reflected about in the previous meditation. The peace which Jesus gives, the peace that is a fruit of the Spirit, is rooted in the conviction that, in the end, all will be well. It is the conviction of David Steindl-Rast "that even the worst, if it happens, will be the best."[1] It is the basic insight of the English mystic Dame Julian of Norwich that "all shall be well; and all manner of thing shall be well."[2] Peace is the inner certainty of the Providence of God.

[1] David Steindl-Rast, *Gratefulness, The Heart of Prayer* (New York: Paulist Press, 1984) 143.

[2] John Skinner (trans.), *Revelation of Love: Julian of Norwich* (New York: Doubleday/Image, 1996) 55.

Horatio G. Spafford had that certainty. "When peace like a river attendeth my way, / when sorrows like sea billows roll; *whatever* my lot," he wrote, "thou hast taught me to say, / it is well . . . with my soul." About 2:00 a.m. the morning of November 22, 1873, the ship the *Ville du Havre*, carrying Spafford's wife and four children to Europe, collided with the English ship *Lochearn*. In the ensuing chaos all four children were lost. Nine days after the shipwreck, Mrs. Spafford cabled her husband, "saved alone." A few hours after the cable reached him Spafford said quietly to a friend, "I am glad to trust the Lord when it will cost me something." Within two years he had lost his livelihood in real estate ventures in the Chicago fire and all his children. And yet as the ship carrying him to reunion with his wife passed near the spot of their calamity, he wrote to his sister, ". . . I do not think of our dear ones there. They are safe, folded, the dear lambs, and there, before very long, shall we be too. In the meantime, thanks to God, we have an opportunity to serve and praise Him for His love and mercy to us and to ours. 'I will praise Him while I have my being.'"[3] Out of the depths of this experience, Spafford wrote the hymn just quoted.

This is one of the most dramatic examples I know of "peace not as the world gives," of what St. Paul called "the peace of God, which surpasses all understanding" (Phil 4:7). It is the serenity that comes from *knowing* that, no matter what happens, all is well because of who God is and what God has done for us. Peace comes from knowing God, not knowing *about* God, but knowing God and God's goodness in spite of human suffering.

And that is why, I think, we love Psalm 23 and turn to it for comfort and sustenance in the very darkest moments of life. It reminds us who God is. It reminds us that God is like a

---

[3] The story is told in chapters 3 and 4 of Bertha Spafford Vester's *Our Jerusalem: An American Family in the Holy City 1881–1949* (Lebanon: Middle East Export Press, Inc., 1950).

good shepherd who provides for, protects, leads, and restores his sheep even in the darkness of death, even in the midst of evil. It reminds us, as we have already considered, that God is good and merciful, and that we shall dwell (note future tense: the tense of promise and hope), we shall dwell (or "abide") in this good God's house forever. Psalm 23 teaches us the nature of God, and knowing that gives us peace.

Of course it is not always so simple. "My ways are not thy ways," says God. "No, joke," is my response. And yet my deepest conviction is that God's ways are always and in every way *better* than my ways, than human ways . . . whether or not I can see it, whether or not I understand it. God does not ask me to understand the Divine ways; God asks me to trust them. And with that trust comes the gift of peace, the peace which *passes* understanding, the peace which guards the heart and mind in Christ Jesus (Phil 4:7).

Peace is the inner certainty of the Providence of God. It says, with Dame Julian of Norwich, "I needs must recognize that all that is done, it is well done, for our Lord does all. . . . Thus I saw truly that I needs must assent with great reverence, simply enjoying in God."[4] Tranquillity of heart comes from knowing God, in fact from having God indwell the heart so completely that the Divine Presence bubbles up and spills over into serenity of mind that allows us to "enjoy in God." "Ask and it will be given; seek and you will find; knock and the door will be opened" (Matt 7:7). God will send the Holy Spirit in the Son's name and the Spirit will teach everything. Peace is Christ's parting gift, a gift of presence, a gift that passes understanding: the knowledge that it is well with the soul.

Peace is Christ's gift to you. Accept it. Take the package home to your heart, and unwrap it there. Rest quietly for a moment and hear the Lord Jesus say to you, "Peace I leave with you; my peace I give to you. . . . Do not let your hearts be troubled, and do not let them be afraid." AMEN.

---

[4] Skinner, *Revelation of Love,* 26, 27.

Joy

Psalm 16

> Protect me, O God, for in you I take refuge.
> > I say to the LORD, "You are my LORD;
> > I have no good apart from you."
> As for the holy ones in the land, they are the noble,
> > in whom is all my delight.
>
> Those who choose another god multiply their sorrows;
> > their drink offerings of blood I will not pour out
> > or take their names upon my lips.
>
> The LORD is my chosen portion and my cup;
> > you hold my lot.
> The boundary lines have fallen for me in pleasant places;
> > I have a goodly heritage.
>
> I bless the LORD who gives me counsel;
> > in the night also my heart instructs me.
> I keep the LORD always before me;
> > because he is at my right hand, I shall not be moved.
>
> Therefore my heart is glad, and my soul rejoices;
> > my body also rests secure.
> For you do not give me up to Sheol,
> > or let your faithful one see the Pit.
> You show me the path of life.
> > In your presence there is fullness of joy;
> > in your right hand are pleasures forevermore.

John 16:20-22

> Very truly, I tell you, you will weep and mourn, but
> the world will rejoice; you will have pain, but your pain
> will turn into joy. When a woman is in labor, she has pain,
> because her hour has come. But when her child is born,
> she no longer remembers the anguish because of the joy of
> having brought a human being into the world. So you
> have pain now; but I will see you again, and your hearts
> will rejoice, and no one will take your joy from you.

"We hold these truths to be self-evident, that all men are created equal, that they are endowed by their Creator with certain unalienable Rights, that among these are Life, Liberty, and the pursuit of Happiness." What on earth could the framers of our Declaration of Independence have had in mind? And I do mean on earth, quite literally.

Now I don't usually quibble with the basic documents of American democracy. I have lived in other places in the world frequently enough and for long enough to know what a fortuitous system we are privileged to enjoy. My problem with the quotation is not its exclusive language: that "men are created equal" by which our founding fathers clearly meant white males. No, my problem is with the idea that the Creator endows us with the right to happiness. That idea, I think, is pure folly. "Happy" isn't a Christian word. It certainly isn't a Christian virtue, and it is not used to describe the nature of God from which, we are assuming, the fruit of the Spirit comes. God is not "happy." Look at the state of the human race. How could God be? "Happy" is an "earthly" and not a "heavenly" or "spiritual" desire. I am sorry to disappoint you, but God didn't make you to be "happy." No, "happy" is a pagan word, pure and simple. Its root word means "chance" or "luck," and it is related to "haphazard, hapless, and happenstance." God loves us too much to endow us only with happiness, to want our hearts to grow in luck. What God wants for us is joy, an enduring, spiritual state, not an ephemeral, emotional one.

This is nowhere so clearly communicated to us as in the farewell discourses of Jesus in John 14–16. The endowments of Jesus to his disciples in these three important chapters are peace and joy. Jesus Christ, and the God he manifests, wants to give us something far more enduring that the ubiquitous "bluebird of happiness." He wants to give us the joy, the abiding delight in life itself, that no one and nothing can take from us.

We all know people, do we not, whom we would have to describe as joyful? These are the people whose eyes have a particular light and sparkle, whose very persons glow from a palpable interior warmth. They may not be, indeed in my experience they usually are not, what could be called "happy" people, the superficial smilers, the "glad handlers," the "hail fellow well met" type, the folks who have been favored by life's circumstances, the universally fortunate. Many, perhaps most, joyful people have faced, survived, and indeed grown from some of life's most difficult circumstances. In their own physical suffering from disease or accident, in the loss of spouse or child, in the reversal of financial circumstances or the loss of material possessions, they are related to the woman in labor in John's text. Their suffering and pain has given birth to new life and permanent joy.

For several years we lived in Germany with its lovely, romantic castles. I very quickly learned that if the family that owned the castle were in residence, their flag flew from the highest tower of the castle. No flag, no family. I have since encountered two versions of a quotation on joy that are related to this flag phenomenon. The first goes like this: "The most infallible proof of the presence of God in a person is joy; it is the flag we fly from our towers when God is in residence in our hearts." And the second is: "Joy is the flag we fly from our countenance when Christ is in residence in our hearts." No flag, no Divine Presence.

Joyful people fly that flag with gusto, don't they? They have a presence and an attitude that is positively contagious. Others see them and want what they have. The interesting question is from whence does this joy come? What is its source, its origin? To put it crassly how do we "get it"? The answer is simple, but it requires a little unpacking. Joy is and comes from gift, from knowing that all life is gift and accepting it as such rather than taking it for granted.

Joy originates, I would suggest, from the root conviction that life itself is a gift, not a given. That is why people who have suffered can become the harbingers of joy. In their suffering they have learned not to take life for granted. Life comes to us as gift. It is the first and most important gift that our parents make to us when they cooperate with God in the generation of babies (itself, in its old-fashioned form, quite a nice process, by the way). We don't have to have it; we didn't have to Be, but we Are. Joy is the proper response of the creature to the Creator. It originates from our own origin in gift. Joy floods in when we recognize the gift-nature of all of life.

The intermediate step, it seems to me, what allows us to experience the joy that God wants to give, the "connector" between God's gift to us and our joy, is gratitude. Our joy comes from our gratitude for what we have been given. In his wonderful book *Gratefulness, the Heart of Prayer,* David Steindl-Rast, O.S.B., writes that "joy is . . . independent of what happens to us." "The root of joy is gratefulness. . . . joy springs from gratefulness. . . . it is gratitude that makes us joyful."[1] "And gratefulness is the measure of our aliveness."[2]

That joy comes from gratitude is not just a psychological truth. It is deeply theological as well, rooted in the very meaning of the word "joy." The word "joy," in Greek *chara,* is most often used to describe joy with its basis in religion, precisely because its foundation is in God. Joy, *chara,* comes from the same root as grace, *charis,* a term which the Reformers fastened on to describe the very origin of our salvation. Joy rests in the grace of God to us.

[1] David Steindl-Rast, *Gratefulness, the Heart of Prayer* (New York: Paulist Press, 1984) 204.

[2] Ibid., 12.

Joy arises in gratitude and issues forth in praise because it recognizes the graciousness, the generosity of God. The psalmist understood this deeply as he writes, "I say to the Lord, 'You are my Lord; / I have no good apart from you'" (16:2). Here is the root of joy in human life, the recognition that, apart from God, we have no "good," with all the rich meanings of that simple word. But the psalmist has chosen this attitude: "The Lord is my *chosen* portion and my cup," he says, "you hold my lot. The boundary lines have fallen for me in pleasant places; I have a goodly heritage" (16:5-6). In his moving book *Man's Search for Meaning*, Victor Frankl eloquently reminds us that the last of human freedoms is freedom to choose our attitude in any given set of circumstances. The sort of person we become results from those choices.

We must allow the gifted nature of life to penetrate our hearts; we must open our hearts again to the grace of God which has been so freely given to us in so many ordinary and extraordinary ways. "Count your blessings," my grandmother used to remind me. She was right, more right than she may have known. For the joy that Christ wants his people to have is found precisely there.

It is little wonder that for thousands of years the Psalms have been the prayer book of God's people. The psalmist always gets it right. "My heart is glad," he sings, "and my soul rejoices; my body also rests secure" (19:9). "You show me the path of life. / In your presence there is fullness of joy; / in your right hand are pleasures forevermore" (16:11).

May we take *these* truths to be self-evident; may we take these words to heart. And may they take root and grow there, and bear fruit, fruit that will last. AMEN.

Love

Psalm 36:5-10

> Your steadfast love, O LORD, extends to the heavens,
>   your faithfulness to the clouds.
> Your righteousness is like the mighty mountains,
>   your judgments are like the great deep;
>   you save humans and animals alike, O LORD.
>
> How precious is your steadfast love, O God!
>   All people take refuge in the shadow of your wings.
> They feast on the abundance of your house,
>   and you give them drink from the river of
>   your delights.
> For with you is the fountain of life;
>   in your light we see light.
>
> O continue your steadfast love to those who know you,
>   and your salvation to the upright of heart!

John 15:9-17

"As the Father has loved me, so I have loved you; abide in my love. If you keep my commandments, you will abide in my love, just as I have kept my Father's commandments and abide in his love. I have said these things to you so that my joy may be in you, and that your joy may be complete.

"This is my commandment, that you love one another as I have loved you. No one has greater love than this, to lay down one's life for one's friends. You are my friends if you do what I command you. I do not call you servants any longer, because the servant does not know what the master is doing; but I have called you friends, because I have made known to you everything that I have heard from my Father. You did not choose me but I chose you. And I appointed you to go and bear fruit, fruit that will last, so that the Father will give you whatever you ask him in my name. I am giving you these commands so that you may love one another."

Somewhere, inscribed in bold letters in the list of Universal Truths, the following statement undoubtedly occurs: "If things can get more complicated, they will." Individuals, families, institutions, societies all have a maddening tendency to get more complex. Anthropologists note that as stories are told and re-told they get longer and more complex. As small businesses grow, their organizational flowcharts get more and more complex. In colleges and universities, administrators proliferate like rabbits (trust me on this one). Bureaucracies seem, like amoeba, to be self-generating. Even Christianity has grown more and more complex with the passage of time. Setting aside the great and often perplexing variety of Christian denominations, Roman Catholic canon law or the Episcopal Church's Rubrics for Worship alone prove the point.

The human species has a genius for making things more difficult, multifarious, and knotty. And that is why this text from Jesus' farewell discourse in the Gospel of John is such a breath of fresh air. It reminds us, as the Lord Jesus reminded Martha in another context, that only one thing is really necessary.

Judaism of the first century had also become complex. A whole body of oral interpretation had been appended to the written requirements of the Torah as it was recorded in the Pentateuch, and both were increasingly binding on observant Jews. Little wonder that a Jerusalem scribe came to Jesus and asked, "Which commandment is the first of all?" Jesus responded in the words of the Shema, the Jewish confession of faith, "The first is, 'Hear oh Israel: the Lord our God, the Lord is one; you shall love the Lord your God with all your heart, and with all your soul, and with all your mind, and with all your strength.' The second is this, 'You shall love your neighbor as yourself.' There is no other commandment greater than these" (Mark 12:28-31).

Cutting through the religious complexity of the day, Jesus declared unequivocally that the crucial command was to love God and neighbor. In John's farewell discourse, just after he has demonstrated what love meant by washing feet, Jesus gave a new commandment: "Just as I have loved you, you also should love one another. By this everyone will know that you are my disciples, if you have love for one another" (John 13:34-35).

The apostle Paul, who never met the earthly Jesus, understood his basic message with crystal clarity. Paul wrote to the church at Rome, "Owe no one anything, except to love one another; for the one who loves another has fulfilled the law." "Love does no wrong to a neighbor; therefore, love is the fulfilling of the law" (Rom 13:8, 10).

A single, four-letter word changes the means of human acceptability to God. For a sacrificial system and a notion of legal rectitude, a simple, relational concept is substituted. What matters to God is not whether I have completed the proper sacrifices or observed the rituals, not whether I am "nice," or "competent," or pious, whether I attend to religious duties, or engage in the religious busy work that is so often substituted for real Christianity. No, what matters to God is whether or not I am a good lover. Central to growth of the heart is repeatedly asking myself the question "am I becoming a more loving person?"

This is a radically new approach to God. Even John the Evangelist cannot quite give up the idea of commandments (and in this he is like us who want to cling to our legalisms), so he explains that followers of Jesus will abide in their Lord's love if they follow his Father's commandments (15:10). And then he drops the other shoe: "This is my commandment, that you love one another as I have loved you" (15:12). *"Love as I have loved you,"* says the Jesus who stands between the foot washing and the cross.

It's all well and good to say "love's the thing." But what do we mean by "love?" "Love" is used forty-three times in 1 John. As that writer understands it, love is not a fleeting emotion, a warm sentiment, an overdose of sexual hormones. No, it is much more serious than those feelings, lovely as they can be. To put the message of 1 John in modern terminology we might say that Christian love is a matter of the will, of deciding to act as God acted in Jesus Christ, and then consistently striving to do so. Love is the unconquerable benevolence that only seeks the good for others and seeks neither consolation nor gain for one's self. As such it usually involves deliberate effort.

John is clear about the origin of "true love." "Love is from God" (1 John 4:7). In fact, love is the essential characteristic of God. Psalm 36 speaks of God's steadfast love. The first letter of John says simply "God *is* love" (4:16b). This is probably the first thing a child learns about God and the most difficult thing for an adult to comprehend about the Divinity. Human love is initiated by God: God "loved us and sent his son to be the atoning sacrifice for our sins" (4:10). "We love because God first loved us" (4:19). This is why the writer of 1 John calls the recipients of his epistle "beloved." They, and we, are the ones who are loved by God. If you retain nothing else from these meditations, remember this one thing: God loves you.

Christian love is not self-generated; God is always its source. We cannot really love when we are left to our own devices. Psychologists tell us we must *be* loved to love. "We love because God first loved us" is profoundly true. Furthermore, love always comes to us as gift. Did you ever try to make somebody love you? I remember with great chagrin my seventh-grade crush, a tall, skinny boy with greasy brown hair and an Adam's apple about the size of a golf ball. I did everything I could to attract his attention . . . which with limp hair, braces on my teeth, and corrective shoes wasn't much. Alas. No flame of love was ignited.

If you have some embarrassing experience of this sort in your past (and frankly I hope you do), then you understand the truth of the gift-nature of love. Real love comes not from human effort, but from Divine disclosure. It cannot be given if it has not been received. We usually first experience it in another's love for us, that amazing and heady experience of *being* loved and knowing we have neither earned nor deserved it. God loves us through others, and we, in turn, learn in this very human way to become the channels of God's love to others.

The nature of that love is extremely serious. It is seen most clearly in the life of Jesus. Because God loved us, God came to us in Jesus of Nazareth to show us how to love. Jesus begins to show us how to love when he, himself, accepts the love of a woman who wipes his feet with her hair. And this may be the hardest task of love for us, not so much to show it ourselves, as to accept it when it comes to us. We see Jesus loving as he sets aside his royal prerogative and stoops to wash the feet of fishermen and accountants and laborers. We see the extent of Jesus' love—how broad and deep and high it is—as he stretches out his arms on a Roman cross in what the Roman Catholic liturgy so beautifully calls "a death he freely accepted." The love we Christians are to have is not an ephemeral well-wishing or a matter of mawkish sentiment. It is the willingness literally to give up ourselves for one another, to stretch out our own arms to embrace the cross and through it, the world. "No one has greater love than this, to lay down one's life for one's friends" (John 15:13) or for strangers, or for enemies.

We whom God so loves are, because of that love, required to love as Jesus loves—to give ourselves up for each other, to die to self that others may have life more abundantly. The cross of Jesus Christ is the bridge of love that God has thrown across our world so that we may transcend the boundaries between us and be made perfect in God. If love is the finest fruit of the Spirit, self-offering is the sweetest part of the fruit. And the wonderful thing is, that as we learn to love as Jesus loved, as we practice doing so, as we desire his heart for our own heart, we experience God's love more and more intensely ourselves. As we love others, we find that we do, indeed, "abide in God and God abides in" us (v. 16).

The essence of the Christian life, its loveliest fruit, is profound but very uncomplicated. It is love: the love of God which called all that exists into being, which fills our world and the people who inhabit it, which is the one abiding virtue and which must animate our every thought, motive, and action. We Christians are called to the very serious business of manifesting a quality of character and life that can only come from God, that is, in fact, God in essence.

Christianity is not as complex as we have made it. It is not denominational politics or loyalties. It is not forms of worship or liturgical correctness. It is not even personal morality as if the Christian faith could be reduced to a sort of moral equivalent of Emily Post or Miss Manners. Christianity is not good works or religious busy work. It is not believing the right things, knowing the right creeds and catechisms, understanding the most complex theological doctrines. Christianity is a relationship which shows forth what God is: love, the source, means, motive, and end of all that ever was, is, or will be. Do not underestimate the power of this love or what it might ask of you. The simple fact of Christian love is not sentimental piety, but the difficult and life-consuming task of integrating our relationship with God and our relationships to others.

During Easter week of A.D. 415 in the North African City of Hippo Regius on the Mediterranean coast, St. Augustine preached line by line through 1 John. He has understood that epistle in great depth. "Once and for all, I give you a short precept," Augustine declared, "Love, and do what you will." And that charge remains our task. AMEN.